SAMUEL BARBER

ADAGIO

arranged for violin and piano
by Jerry Lanning

(score and part)

ED 3995

First printing: May 1996

G. SCHIRMER, Inc.

DISTRIBUTED BY
HAL•LEONARD®
CORPORATION
7777 W. BLUEMOUND RD. P.O. BOX 13819 MILWAUKEE, WI 53213

ADAGIO

Samuel Barber Op. 11

arranged by Jerry Lanning

SAMUEL BARBER

ADAGIO

arranged for violin and piano
by Jerry Lanning

Violin

ED 3995
First printing: May 1996

G. SCHIRMER, *Inc.*

DISTRIBUTED BY
HAL•LEONARD®
CORPORATION
7777 W. BLUEMOUND RD. P.O. BOX 13819 MILWAUKEE, WI 53213

VIOLIN

ADAGIO

Samuel Barber Op. 11
arranged by Jerry Lanning

Tempo I

Tempo I

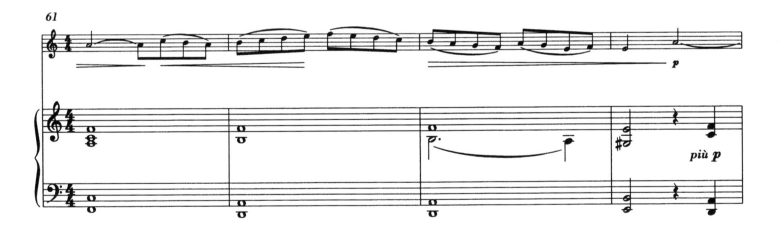

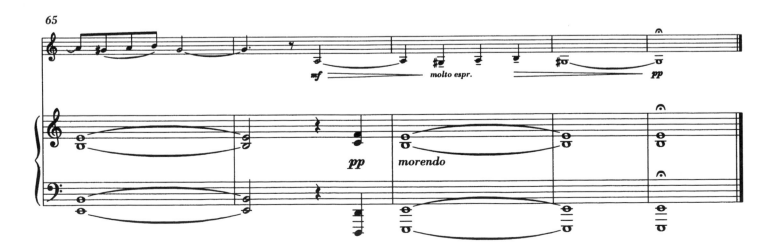